THE ORPHAN TRAINS

Essential Events

THE ORPHAN TRAINS

BY KRISTIN F. JOHNSON

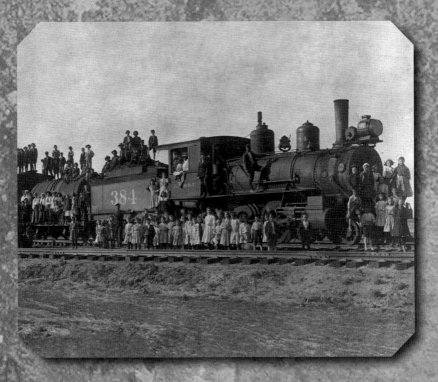

Content Consultant
Dr. Richard Aquila
Professor of History
Penn State University, Erie

ABDO
Publishing Company

CREDITS

Published by ABDO Publishing Company, PO Box 398166, Minneapolis, MN 55439. Copyright © 2012 by Abdo Consulting Group, Inc. International copyrights reserved in all countries. No part of this book may be reproduced in any form without written permission from the publisher. The Essential Library™ is a trademark and logo of ABDO Publishing Company.

Printed in the United States of America,
North Mankato, Minnesota
092011
012012

 THIS BOOK CONTAINS AT LEAST 10% RECYCLED MATERIALS.

Editor: Mari Kesselring
Copy Editor: Rebecca Rowell
Cover Design: Kazuko Collins
Interior Design and Production: Marie Tupy

Library of Congress Cataloging-in-Publication Data
Johnson, Kristin F., 1968-
  The orphan trains / by Kristin F. Johnson.
      p. cm. -- (Essential events)
  Includes bibliographical references.
  ISBN 978-1-61783-103-4
  1. Orphan trains--United States--History--Juvenile literature.
2. Orphans--United States--History--Juvenile literature. I.
Title.
  HV985.J64 2011
  362.734--dc22
                                        2011009544

TABLE OF CONTENTS

A group of orphans ready to board a train

DIRE CONDITIONS

*I*n New York City in the early 1850s,
approximately 30,000 homeless children
roamed the streets. Many had been born into
families that suffered from a variety of issues,
including poverty, crime, disease, alcoholism, and

hunger. Some children's parents had died from those problems. Other parents could no longer care for their children because of poverty or poor health, so they abandoned them. Abandoned children sometimes lived on the streets. Orphan Elliot Bobo explained that he was taken in by the Children's Aid Society (CAS) for two of those reasons: "Far as I know, my father hit the bottle pretty heavy and they took us away from him. And my mother died when I was two years old."[1]

Another orphan, Claretta Miller, looked back on her experience when she was much older. She recalled the difficulties of her family life before the orphan train relocated her:

House of Refuge

In 1825, the New York State House of Refuge was opened. The institution housed children who had committed crimes, such as theft, selling stolen goods, drunkenness, and gambling. These offenses were reason enough for a homeless child to be sent to the House of Refuge.

We were hungry. I don't ever recall taking a bath in a tub of water. We slept on old, dirty mattresses on the floor and the rats ran over our heads and through our hair lots of nights and we'd wake up screaming with it. We don't know where our parents were. We never did know.[2]

The police and other agencies often discovered children who needed homes, sometimes because the children committed crimes. Homeless children would be placed in institutions called children's asylums, workhouses, or almshouses. These places were overcrowded and unsanitary, and they treated people more like caged animals than humans. Charles Loring Brace, who had founded the CAS in 1853, felt these institutions were no place for children because they were a breeding ground for future criminals. He wanted to take children from these bad influences and give them a chance at productive and happy lives. So, Brace began the orphan train movement, which would send children west by train, away from the big port cities of the eastern United States in hopes of giving them a better future. In western homes and on farms, the children could be placed with families who wanted them and could afford to take care of them. In return, the children would help with farming.

ALL ABOARD

On September 28, 1854, the first group of children to ride an orphan train left New York City for the Midwest. The children hoped to be adopted by families there. "I had the whole future ahead of me," Bobo recalled, "and I didn't know what to expect, but I didn't want to stay in the orphanage."[3]

Three adults from the CAS accompanied 37 boys and girls between the ages of six and 15 on the trip. First, the group rode a boat to Albany, New York. There, they picked up nine more children then boarded a train for the longer journey west. This first orphan train would travel for approximately four days to the small town of Dowagiac, Michigan. Orphan Lee Nailling summed up his feelings at the time:

I do remember the children milling around outside the train, waiting to be assigned our seats. The big problem was that you never knew what the future held for you. You had no idea what the future ever held for you and that was a great concern and a great worry.[4]

Farming in the Midwest

In 1854, farming was a booming trade. Farming communities were in rural regions, mostly in the Midwest, where the soil was fertile and the climate was right for farming. Although several new farming technologies made it easier to get more work done with fewer people, farmers still needed workers for many tasks. This created an opportunity for the orphans to relocate to a home where they could contribute to the livelihood of the farm family.

No documentation was left stating why Michigan was selected as the first stop for that orphan train in 1854, but Michigan was the nation's leading producer of wheat. The state was also a leader in lumber industry. The railroads brought orphans to Michigan, but they also allowed Michigan to distribute products such as wheat, lumber, and livestock to other states.

Rags to Riches

Most of the children aboard the first train had been carefully selected for the journey. But one orphan was found the day of departure and brought along for the expedition. The 12-year-old boy was named Liverpool, after the city in England where he had been born. He had come to the United States on a ship where he worked as a cabin boy. Once he got to New York, he worked odd jobs to make money. When he was found, his clothes were old sailor's clothes that were too big and hung off of him. The CAS agent who discovered Liverpool said that "he had so many garments wrapped and tied about his body that he looked like a 'walking rag bundle.'"[5]

The journey was difficult for many of the young travelers. Claretta Miller later explained her experience:

"A company of orphan children under the auspices of the Children's Aid Society of New York will arrive at Valley Falls, Thursday afternoon, December 8. These children are bright, intelligent and well disciplined, both boys and girls of various ages. They are placed on trial, and if not satisfactory will be removed. Parties taking them must be well recommended. A local committee of citizens of Valley Falls has been selected to assist the agents in placing the children. Applications must be made to and endorsed by the local committee. Bring your recommendations with you. . . . Distribution will take place at the opera house, on Friday, December 9, at 10 a.m. and 2 p.m."[6]
—Oskaloosa Independent, *on December 9, 1910*

Homeless boys sleeping in a New York City alley

I had left everything behind. . . . I didn't have my sister anymore. I didn't have my parents anymore. I didn't have any friends. They were total strangers. It just caught up with me all at once. . . . That's when I began to cry was when—the emotion hit me, I think, when I went to get into bed. I still felt all alone and yet I knew there was someone around me, but they were strangers.[7]

On the boat ride to Albany, the children had emigrant tickets—the cheapest tickets for the ride. They were supposed to sleep in the smelly, vermin-infested lowest deck of the boat. They would be crowded together and uncomfortable. However, the captain of the ship, at the last moment, heard the orphans singing and invited the enchanting children to join him in his salon. After hearing several of their sad life stories, the captain arranged for better sleeping space for the children.

ALL THEY OWNED

The CAS provided each child with a small cardboard suitcase for the trip. In their suitcases, the orphans had to carry everything they owned, which usually amounted to little. Each child was also given a Bible as a means of comfort. Years later, Bobo remembered his suitcase:

> *I've kept this suitcase as a souvenir all these years. Each one of us had one. And I don't suppose it was very expensive, not over a couple of bucks, but—we had the handle here we could carry it by. I had all my possessions in there, which wasn't much, just clothes—no shoes, just a change of clothes.*[8]

HOMES WANTED FOR CHILDREN

A notice was sent to the people in Dowagiac about a month ahead of the train's arrival, stating that homes were wanted for children. This allowed time for those in need of workers or in want of children to consider the option of the orphan train children. Some children were adopted right away. Others became indentured servants who would work for farmers until they turned 18. Before the children got off the train, their faces were washed and clothes changed. The CAS wanted the children to make as good of a first impression on prospective parents as possible.

The train to Dowagiac was the first of many to carry orphans from East Coast cities such as New York to Midwest farms. The orphan trains ran for 75 years and relocated approximately 250,000 children in all. Successes and failures followed the orphan train placements. The

Riding the Train

The first orphan train riders traveled in nothing more than cattle cars for the cross-country journey. Though they did have seats, the ride was uncomfortable and crowded. Journeys lasted three or four days, during which time the children slept in their seats and never left the train. Over the years, train accommodations improved. Some of the later riders had much more comfortable conditions for transport—some even got tickets for sleeper cars.

movement is considered the beginning of formal adoption and foster care programs in the United States. And it began with the idea of one man: Charles Loring Brace.

*Brace hoped that the orphan trains
would rescue homeless children from the streets.*

Charles Loring Brace, 1890

CHARLES LORING BRACE

harles Loring Brace was born in Litchfield, Connecticut, on June 19, 1826. When he was 15 years old he attend a sermon by Horace Bushnell. Brace was so moved that he decided he wanted to become a minister. He studied theology at Yale University. After graduating from Yale, he taught briefly in Connecticut and then went back to Yale and attended divinity school for a year. In 1849, he became an ordained minister. Then, Bushnell became Brace's mentor. Bushnell's ideas about how even the smallest actions influence the human soul long-term, especially the souls of children, influenced Brace. Bushnell preached that children are greatly influenced by what goes on around them. In one of Bushnell's sermons, he explained,

> *The child looks and listens, and whatsoever tone of feeling or manner of conduct is displayed around him, sinks into his plastic, passive soul, and becomes a mold of his being ever after. . . . [Children] watch us every moment, in the family, before the hearth, and at the table; and when we are meaning them no good or evil, when we are conscious of exerting no influence over them, they are drawing from us impressions and molds of habit, which, if wrong, no heavenly discipline can wholly remove; or, if right, no bad associations utterly dissipate.* [1]

MOVING TO NEW YORK

In 1848, Brace moved to New York City to study for a life in the ministry at Union Theological

Seminary. He also volunteered at several missions in town. One of these missions was one in the worst slums in the country at the time: Five Points.

By the mid-1800s, New York City was booming with population growth. In 1826, the Erie Canal opened, making New York the main channel for immigrants and trade happening on the East Coast. According to author Stephen O'Connor, "throughout the remainder of the 1800s nearly 1,000 people a day poured into Manhattan."[2] With so many people suddenly living in the urban areas, New York was becoming overpopulated and run-down. The conditions Brace saw around the city appalled him. The population continued to increase dramatically for several decades. According to census reporting, there were 33,131 inhabitants of Manhattan in 1790. By 1890, that number was approximately 1.5 million.

"When a child of the streets stands before you in rags, with a tear-stained face, you cannot easily forget him. And yet, you are perplexed what to do. The human soul is difficult to interfere with. You hesitate how far you should go."[3]
—*Charles Loring Brace*

A clipping from a London newspaper shows an artist's rendering of prisoners on Blackwell's Island in New York City.

At 23 years old, Brace began serving as the preacher for Blackwell's Island in New York. This is where the ill, the criminals, and the poor were housed. Initially, Brace focused on preaching about God and how everyone can make a difference. But he was not seeing results from that work. Poverty, crime, and other serious issues kept growing, and the homeless children continued to crowd the streets of New York.

FALTERING FAITH IN RELIGION

After Brace's regular visits to Blackwell's Island started, he stopped writing to his friend Fred Kingsbury about having a career in the ministry. Instead, he made statements about the "inefficiency of religion."[4] Brace also wrote about how he wanted to do something more to combat the problems of crime and homelessness, especially for the children, but he did not know what that something was. However, he did conclude, "The effort to reform adults was well-nigh hopeless."[5]

Blackwell's Island

Nearly two miles (3 km) long, Blackwell's Island sits between Queens and Manhattan in New York City. In 1828, the Department of Charities and Corrections bought the island from the Blackwell family to house the growing population of criminals and sick people. Because the island was surrounded by treacherous tides, escape was difficult. At the time of the orphan train movement, four structures occupied the island: a madhouse, a hospital for those who could not afford health care, the almshouse to provide food and shelter for those who were destitute, and a workhouse for petty criminals. The workhouse had 756 stone cells designed to house one inmate apiece, but overcrowding resulted in each cell often housing two or three inmates. The hospital, Charity Hospital, had a children's ward that writer and abolitionist Lydia Maria Child described:

[It was] the most painful sight I ever witnessed. About one hundred and fifty children were there, mostly orphans, inheriting every variety of disease from vicious and sickly parents. . . . The poor, little, pale, shriveled, and blinded creatures were waiting for death to come and release them. Here the absence of a mother's love was most agonizing.[6]

A Tragedy

As Brace was pondering these problems, his only sibling, Emma, became ill with tuberculosis (TB). She was sent to the countryside to recover. But Emma's stay in the country did not help, and she died in 1850. Brace was devastated. He grieved and secluded himself for three days. He emerged with a purpose: he would renew his soul through work by traveling to Europe. His two best friends—brothers Frederick Law Olmsted and John Olmsted—joined him.

Trip to Europe

While in Europe, Brace toured German foster care facilities and thought again of the homeless children wandering New York. His faith in preaching to people about doing good works was still faltering. He wanted to find a way to effect change instead of just preaching about it.

In Belfast, Ireland, the men stayed with Robert Neill, an activist who was against slavery in the United States. Brace met Letitia, Neill's daughter, and spent a lot of time walking with her and discussing religion. Brace left Neill's house to continue his trip but later returned and continued to see Letitia. The couple talked about getting married.

Visiting the Rough House

From there, Brace returned to Germany. He was writing a column for a newspaper back home called the *Independent*. In one column, he wrote that there was a need for a "revival in home life" not a "revival in religion."[7] Brace also visited a German orphanage called *Rauhe Haus,* or "Rough House." But this German institution was nothing like the asylums in New York. The Rough House was in the country and resembled a farm. Children there performed labor similar to that of farmworkers in the United States. Brace thought the children were closer to God in Germany because they were working among nature while farming. Brace thought the Rough House was superior to New York's asylums.

Letter to Emma

Just two days before Emma died, Brace wrote her a letter in which he shared news of New York and stated the problem he would spend the rest of his career combating: "New York is whirling on as usual. You can have no idea, Emma, what an immense vat of misery and crime and filth much of this great city is! I realize it more and more. Think of *ten thousand children* growing up almost sure to be prostitutes and rogues!"[8]

ARRESTED IN HUNGARY

After touring Germany, Brace went to Hungary. On May 24, 1851, while dining at a friend's house, Brace was arrested. Initially, the police claimed Brace was arrested for not handing in his traveling papers, which consisted of official Austrian government documents, for review. Later, he was told the arrest was actually because Brace was investigating the workings of Hungarian institutions. Brace had been vocal about his views on politics and that he opposed the ways of the Hungarian government. The Hungarian police thought Brace was there to conspire with revolutionaries and jailed him. The jail was in an old castle. Brace was imprisoned with Hungarian revolutionaries. Being in the Hungarian jail was harrowing for Brace. He was under constant threat of being beaten up or worse and did not know when he would get out, if ever.

Brace's friend Eljen McCurdy worked with the US consul in Hungary to obtain Brace's release. After being held prisoner for almost one month, Brace was set free on June 21, 1851, two days after his birthday. Brace returned to the United States and spent time at Frederick Olmsted's farm, where he wrote more about improving the lives of poor children. He also wrote about how the revolutionaries he had met in jail affected him: "I resolved inwardly that, God willing, my efforts should never fail, while I had strength to give them, for the oppressed in any land."[9]

Farming as an Ideal

Olmsted repeatedly told Brace how peaceful he felt working on his Staten Island farm, how close to God he felt, and how much work there was to be done. This, combined with what Brace witnessed at the Rough House in Germany, gave him a new idea.

Brace wondered if he could send poor orphans to live with farm families. The orphans would learn a valuable skill and could become part of a family unit in which they would be cared for and loved. Sending the orphans away from the crime and street gangs of New York would

Frederick Olmsted

Frederick Olmsted was one of Brace's best friends. In 1848, Olmsted moved to a farm on the south side of Staten Island. The farm helped inspire Brace's plans to send orphans west. Later in Olmsted's career, he co-designed New York City's Central Park and Prospect Park with his business partner, Calvert Vaux. In 1858, Olmsted and Vaux entered a design contest for Central Park and won. Central Park construction was finished in 1873.

also protect the children from the bad influences that Bushnell had preached about. Brace hoped this would be a better life for the orphans and lead to a better future than that in New York.

Founding the Children's Aid Society

In 1853, Brace solicited the financial backing of reformers, civic leaders, and businessmen to start an organization that would help impoverished and orphaned children. With this support, Brace founded the Children's Aid Society (CAS). His goals for the organization would prove challenging and ongoing. In his *New York Times* column, "Walks Among the New-York Poor," he wrote, "The means of help must be as continuous as are the sources of evil."[10] Setting up the CAS would provide a means for fighting the evils of society—alcoholism, vagrancy,

"Walks Among the New-York Poor" Column

Brace wrote a column for the *New York Times* that literally reflected him walking among the poor in the worst areas of New York, such as Five Points and the Eleventh Ward. Brace reported on what he called the "dangerous classes," which included criminals, vagabonds, and prostitutes and the poor living conditions in the tenements. In one column, Brace stated, "The Press now is the pulpit," reflecting on how he decided he could reach masses of people more effectively through the media than by preaching in church to a congregation.[11]

crime, and disease—in the children's favor. But no one knew just how long the fight would last.

Brace wanted to help homeless children.

Immigrants underwent medical inspections before they were permitted to enter the United States.

HOMELESS CHILDREN

In the early 1850s, New York City was booming with people from foreign lands searching for a better life and new opportunities. Some parts of the country were quickly becoming overcrowded, especially port cities such as New York and Boston. Immigrants were looking for work, but New York's industries were not expanding at the same pace as the number of immigrants flooding into the city.

LIFE OF THE POOR

Many of the existing jobs were with family-owned businesses that employed only their own family members. Therefore, immigrants often could not break into the job market unless they were taken on as apprentices to learn a trade. Immigrants rarely wanted to take apprenticeships because they would not be paid. The lack of jobs left many immigrants hungry, homeless, and desperate. Every day was a struggle for the poor to stay fed, housed, and alive. Poverty became so bad that people could not afford to feed and shelter their children. For many, crime became a way of survival. According to one newspaper article of the time, the crime problem could be boiled down to this:

Statue of Liberty

Upon arriving in the United States by ship, the Statue of Liberty was the first sight immigrants would usually see as they neared land. The statue was a gift to the United States from France in 1886. "The New Colossus," a poem by Emma Lazarus, was inscribed on the statue: "Give me your tired, your poor, Your huddled masses yearning to breathe free, The wretched refuse of your teeming shore. Send these, the homeless, tempest-tossed to me. I lift my lamp beside the golden door."[1]

Many of them who were willing to work could find no work to do, and with the two great prompters to evil— hunger and idleness—constantly at hand, they could not easily be restrained from falling into vice.[2]

Five Points was the worst area of the city for crime. Oddly, it was within blocks of one of the best areas of the city: the ritzy and booming Broadway. But in Five Points, the homeless wandered the streets and begged on every corner. The streets themselves contrasted with Broadway's orderly cobblestone. The mud-based streets of Five Points were filthy with pig and horse manure—enough that a person's feet could sink into the muck while walking. Taverns and food markets were the only businesses that flourished. The biggest problems in Five Points were drunkenness, prostitution, and violence. Gangs also thrived there.

Living conditions were another problem. Poor families were mostly housed in tenements. These small, low-income apartments had just one

Tuberculosis

Tuberculosis (TB), also known as consumption, is caused by bacteria that usually attack the lungs. At the time of the orphan train movement, TB was one of the leading causes of death among New Yorkers. TB spreads through air when an infected person coughs or sneezes. Oddly, the disease is not spread by touching hands, kissing, or even sharing food or drink with an infected person. Today, TB is still a problem, and the World Health Organization is working to battle drug-resistant strains of the disease.

*A policeman leads an upper-class group
through the Five Points neighborhood.*

or two rooms. Tenets shared an outdoor bathroom.
In some cases, as many as 15 people might end up all
living in one room together. The close and usually
unsanitary conditions provided the perfect breeding
ground for germs that spread diseases rapidly.
Rodents were another problem that added to the
quick spread of disease.

Many people died in the poor, rat-infested
tenements from diseases such as TB, cholera, typhus,
yellow fever, trachoma (an eye disease), and favus
(a scalp disease). Because modern medicine, such as

penicillin, and cures had not yet been discovered, many parents who became ill died, leaving their children to fend for themselves.

Future Criminals

One place the government saw to move criminals and other undesirables, such as orphans, was to Blackwell's Island. However, even the superintendent of the prison had doubts about the effectiveness of the remote island as a solution to societal ills. He told Lydia Maria Child, a writer and activist, about his doubts once when she toured the facilities. She later explained, "Ten years' experience had convinced him that the whole system tended to increase crime."[3] Brace had noticed that most of the many young people who had been on the island ended up in Sing Sing, an adult prison just north of New York City. He thought that an environment such as Blackwell's Island could not help troubled children change their negative behaviors.

Meanwhile, crime and mortality rates in New York City kept rising. Conditions worsened as the population grew with the influx of people. An estimated 30,000 children wandered the city's streets. Though laws were being passed to address children's education, many of the children did not attend school.

Many poor or homeless children became beggars for food and money, some became thieves. These latter problems of poverty and thievery were of great concern to the community and to Brace. He wanted to get these children on a righteous path. In one of his column's early articles, Brace said this of homeless boys,

But no one befriends them, or puts them in the right way, and for most of the time, they must struggle, either by good or bad means, to make a living.[4]

If children were caught stealing or causing trouble, they were sent to orphan asylums, almshouses, and workhouses. Typically, children were treated roughly at these

Young Violence

Without adults to teach them how to behave and to set an example for settling arguments with peers, some street children turned to violence. A juvenile crime reported in the *New York Times* on May 26, 1869, illustrates this problem. The article "A Juvenile Stabbing Affray" depicts violence between children:

THOMAS MARRIE, of No. 134 Mott-street, and several other boys were playing marbles in Benson-street yesterday afternoon, when PATRICK SULLIVAN, of No. 55 Mulberry-street, stole some of the marbles and ran off. He was pursued by young MARRIE, and being overtaken by him, he turned and stabbed his prisoner in the arm with a penknife, causing two severe wounds. The boy was subsequently arrested, and on being brought before Justice DOWLING, at the Tombs, he was held for trial.[5]

institutions. They were often forced to work long hours with few breaks. Misbehaving could result in beatings, whippings, and other harsh punishments. However, lawmakers believed these large establishments were the best available solution. While some people felt bad for the orphans and recognized the problem, they were still unable to come up with a better solution.

Some children found jobs on the street to help support themselves or their families. Many children would sell items such as matches, newspapers, or even rags. There was a fairly large population of children known as newsboys, mostly boys and a few girls, who sold newspapers to make a living. But even working children did not always have a place to sleep at the end of their long work day. Providing a warm bed for these working children would be Brace's first goal.

Child Labor Laws

In 1904, the National Child Labor Committee formed and attempted but was unsuccessful in lobbying to end child labor. This failure was partly due to the fact that they were trying to prohibit children from entering into labor contracts. Later, Congress proposed a constitutional amendment but failed. Finally, in 1938, after the Great Depression ended, President Franklin Delano Roosevelt passed the Fair Labor Standards Act. This prohibited employment of children under 14 years of age. It also placed restrictions on young workers between the ages of 14 and 17. Once the act became law, adults did not have to compete with children for jobs. However, not all types of child labor were covered in the act. Children continued to work in fields picking beans and other crops not covered or regulated by provisions of this act.

*Lydia Maria Child was mainly involved in abolition causes,
but she was also concerned about the well-being of children.*

Newsboys selling papers near the Brooklyn Bridge in 1908

NEWSBOYS
AND LODGING HOUSES

efore the CAS began sending children
west to be adopted, Brace found
another class of children he wanted to help. They
were young workers, mostly boys, with two main
areas of occupation: newsboys and bootblacks, or

shoe shiners. Working earned them money and, therefore, freedom. But Brace recognized what most of those children did not: there was no real future for them in those industries once they grew up. Some of the children were orphans, but more of them came from poor families without the means to care for them. So the children set out at early ages, most ranging from six to 15 years old, usually with little adult supervision.

There was great demand for newsboys, especially in New York, because there were so many newspapers in circulation. As early as the 1830s, Benjamin Day, the *New York Sun* editor, had the idea of using young boys who were poor to sell his newspapers on the street. This way, Day felt he could get an edge on the competition because "poor boys would make the best salesmen, since they would not ask for much money and, despite their shabbiness, would not be as threatening as equally shabby grown men."[1]

The most popular papers to sell, which were also going through a bitter rivalry, were the *Journal* and *New York World*. The newsboys, or newsies, gathered at Newspaper Row in Manhattan each day to pick up papers around 4:00 or 5:00 a.m. Then, they went out to their usual beats to sell the papers on street corners. The first newsies in line would get their papers faster and be the first ones selling. The fact that unsold papers could not be returned also provided incentive for rising early and selling hard, including running up and down streets yelling out the day's headlines to prospective customers. Sales for the day would often end around 9:00 a.m. The newsies would then use their profits, approximately twenty-eight cents for selling a full bundle of 56 papers, to have a pancake breakfast and coffee, which cost nine cents. Then, the newsies might go about working at other odd jobs, such as carrying suitcases for passengers boarding the ferry, where they might make more money for lunch.

A Rough Life

At the end of the workday, most newsboys had no home to go to. This was not necessarily because they were

Bootblacks

Another group of working boys was the bootblacks. These boys shined shoes to earn money. They had a captain in charge of their group and had to pay the captain a portion of their wages. In the cold winter months, some bootblacks set up shop above steel grates in the sidewalk. The grates released warm steam from below, a welcome relief from the cold in the winter.

Like newsboys, bootblacks were poor boys who worked on the street.

orphans. In fact, there were many reasons why they were homeless. Some ran away from abusive homes to try to make a better life. Others had families that could not provide for them. Newsboys often slept in boxes or alleys and around steam grates for the warm air. Some newsboys did not have winter coats and went barefoot selling newspapers.

What disturbed Brace was what the newsboys might grow up to become. When Brace toured some tenements in New York, he saw older former newsboys sitting in back rooms drunk. Unable to convince young newsboys of their future fate, Brace wanted to find a way to help them.

Lodging Houses

In 1854, the CAS built its first lodging house for these working city boys on the top floor of the *New York Sun*'s building. This initial lodge, Newsboys' Lodging House, accommodated nearly 50 boys. Shortly after the first lodging house was built, Brace came up with the idea of orphan trains. However, only

---

Newspapers of New York

During the orphan train movement, the interest in news and newspapers was high because of the population growth due to the Industrial Revolution and immigrants coming to the United States. There were several papers printed in foreign languages used by immigrants. In 1843, just before the start of the orphan train movement, Richard March Hoe invented the rotary printing press, which allowed continuous printing from large paper rolls. This made printing quicker and cheaper than before. By 1870, New York City alone had 90 papers.

Not all the children who sold newspapers were boys.
Newsgirls also sold papers.

a portion of the newsboys were willing to leave the
city for the risk of living a farm life that was unknown
to them. Many newsboys were happy with their daily

work life and evenings gambling and going to plays, and sleeping at the lodging house. As Brace began to organize and run orphan trains, he continued to operate lodging houses for poor and homeless children.

In 1858, a new lodging house with 250 beds was opened for boys. In 1862, a lodging house for girls was opened. The cost of lodging was six cents per day, which bought breakfast, supper, and a bed. Their meals included hearty foods, such as stews, bread, and butter. The boys drank coffee and tea. The lodge also provided prayer services and taught skilled labor courses to prepare some of the boys for a home out west. Every two weeks, the CAS would select some boys from the lodging house to send west.

Improving Futures

Eventually, part of Brace's goal for the boys in the lodging house was to create opportunities for them through education. If the boys did not want to move away from New York City, then Brace would find a way to improve their future in the city. Brace opened industrial schools in the lodging house and provided night classes for the boys, knowing most could not attend classes while selling their newspapers during the daytime. Some of the classes offered were for skilled tradesmen's jobs such as shoemakers and mechanics. Brace stayed consistent throughout his work and programs in his efforts to train workers rather than give them handouts.

One night in 1875, a former newsboy came to speak to the children at the Newsboys' Lodging House. He had gone west on an orphan train and been employed by a farmer in Indiana. He told of his life before going west:

Newsboys Go on Strike

The way newsboys worked was to pay the paper distributor for a bundle of papers, then sell the papers on a designated street corner. In 1898, however, the two largest publishers—William Randolph Hearst, publisher of *The New York Journal*, and Joseph Pulitzer, publisher of the *New York World*—raised the price they charged the newsboys in an effort to reduce losses for themselves. Stories had begun to dry up after the Spanish-American War ended. As sales went down, so did profits. But the newsboys would not accept the reduced wages.

On July 22, 1899, the newsboys organized a union and went on strike against those two publishers. Newsies demanded that distributors reduce the amount they charged to the prewar rate. The newsboys posted banners on lampposts pleading for people to support them and boycott buying these papers. The organized efforts of the newsboys' strike took both tycoons off guard. Memos reported the worsening conditions of the strike to Pulitzer: "The newsboys strike has grown into a menacing affair. . . . It is proving a serious problem. Practically all the boys in New York and adjacent towns have quit selling."[2]

The strike went on for two weeks, until Pulitzer and Hearst eventually admitted defeat and offered a compromise. They would keep the same rate but take back unsold papers.

Sometimes I stole things. . . . I would turn in [for the night] in a box, and one winter night I was snuggled up in a box and nearly froze. . . . The fact was I was growing up a thief and a vagabond, and my parents weren't of much good to me. When my father came home at midnight, drunk, he used to beat me black and blue with the end of his strap, and strike my mother till she foamed at the mouth. [3]

The boy who had spoken to them had made a successful new start for himself in farming and was now studying to be a minister. The boy was so convincing that several boys showed up at the CAS office the next day and asked to be sent west as well. This was exactly the effect Brace wanted. Because of the personal testimony of one former newsboy who took an orphan train west, more boys were willing to take that same chance for a new start away from New York City. From the point of view of Brace and the CAS, even if the newsboys were not truly orphans, the change of circumstances was going to give them a better life. The orphan trains were the key to new opportunities.

The Newsboys' Lodging House

*The railroad was still a new form of transportation
when Brace began the orphan trains.*

THE SOLUTION:
ORPHAN TRAINS

race and the CAS came up with a simple solution to the problem of homeless children: give them homes. Brace felt that orphan trains were a better solution than the lodging houses he had helped run. Brace also wanted to educate the children so they could take care of themselves as adults. He did not think charity meant a lack of labor or a handout. Instead, he thought charity meant helping one get work or learn a new skill to regain one's independence. In an 1854 newspaper column he wrote,

> The worst evils in the world are not hunger, and cold, and nakedness. It is far worse to see self-reliance weakened, manliness sapped, and a family growing up only to depend.[1]

Brace first planned to help homeless children by founding industrial schools in lodging houses where children would learn trades that would allow them to work and earn a living. His other idea was to send children far away from the temptations to commit crime in the city. Brace believed true reform only had a chance of being successful if the reform plan included action. The action he felt was most important in this case was to drastically change the child's circumstances.

Parents

In his "Walks Among the New-York Poor" column, Brace quoted one woman whose husband had been killed in a street fight. The woman's son looked weak and Brace offered to get him work in the country, but the woman said, "No niver; shure and isn't he all I have in the wurld? . . . but I cannot part with him, God Bless him!"[2] Some children were in the worst conditions, but the parents loved them or needed their help and could not part with their children even if it meant a chance at a better life.

The Railroad

Brace hoped to give orphans a new start in homes far away from the poverty, disease, and corruption that plagued their lives in New York City. This change became possible because of the westward expansion of the railroad. Had it not been for this advance in transportation, the orphan trains would never have existed.

At the time, train transport was the cheapest way to travel. A child could ride the train for $12 to $15. This was a bargain compared to the costs the CAS might incur caring for the child in New York, which would include food, clothes, and lodging. Moving children to homes in the country was known as placing-out.

A Change of Circumstances

According to Brace, the orphan train riders fell into one of three classes of children:

Powering the Trains

A combination of coal and steam was used to fuel the locomotive trains the orphans rode. During the Industrial Revolution, between the middle of the eighteenth century and the middle of the nineteenth century, coal was popular because it was the most readily available source of fuel. Ash from the coals caused the faces of the orphan train children to become filthy on the train rides. As a result, one of the first things done when arriving in one of the placement towns was to wash the children's faces.

First, the children of destitute parents, whose destitution surrounds them constantly with temptation; second, vagrants—runaways from decent homes, beggars, or at times engaged in some of the minor industries; and third, actual criminals.[3]

One example of a child working in a minor industry was a newsboy. Brace wrote about this type of boy in his column. The boy was lodging in a place where the landlord asked the boys, his tenants, to do errands and then rewarded the boys with a drink of rum and brandy. This indulgence was paving the way for the boys to be future alcoholics if they were not taken out of those conditions.

Other train riders were selected for reasons Brace did not specify. Some were selected if a parent became too ill to care for the child. Others had already been moved to lodging houses run by the CAS. In the early days of placement, Brace and other CAS workers also looked for prospective children on the streets of New York.

Orphans?

One criticism of the orphan trains was that the CAS program separated families in which the parents and other siblings were still alive. Not all train riders were orphans. In fact, one report showed that in 1873, 40 percent of the 3,000 children placed by the CAS still had one or both parents living.

The CAS always got permission in writing from the parents to relocate the children, but it was not always made clear to parents and children that they would no longer have contact with each other. Additionally, immigrant parents may not have clearly understood English. They might not have realized that the relocation was

Westward Railroad Expansion

At the same time immigration was booming through New York City, the railroad was expanding across the United States. Small towns sprang up along the tracks. These towns became the gateways for orphans in the placing-out process. The first orphan trains rode along the shorter railway lines that were the only ones available at the time. The orphans crossed New York by train from Albany to Buffalo. The orphans then took a boat ride from Buffalo across Lake Erie to Michigan, where they boarded another train to reach their first placing-out city: Dowagiac.

Initially, investors did not want to take a chance on further railroad expansion because it was risky. But the government knew an intercontinental system running north to south and east to west was needed for the country to be cohesive. Things changed on July 1, 1862, when President Abraham Lincoln signed the important Pacific Rail Act of 1862 into law. It approved government funding to build a railroad between the Missouri River and California, but there was still a lack of money. Once private investors were found, the tracks were built. Eventually, orphan trains delivered children to 47 of the 48 existing states.

permanent and that they might never see their child again.

Lee Nailling reported that his biological father sent him on the train with an envelope that included his father's contact information so the two could stay in touch. Nailling said he kept the envelope carefully guarded in his coat pocket, but after his first night riding the train, he could not find the envelope. When he was searching for the envelope, he remembered that one of the CAS chaperones accompanying the train told him "to get up, get in my seat, where I was going I would not need that envelope."[4]

This type of deliberate disconnection perhaps created one of the greatest hardships for families who later wanted to reconnect. When the CAS placed children, they never changed the child's name; however, the adoptive parents often did change the names of children they took in. New parents often changed a child's religion, too. In an article for *Ancestry Magazine*, author Marilyn Holt wrote,

> Children taken by the New York Foundling Hospital were baptized in the Catholic Church and placed in Catholic homes. Said a woman who was given up as an infant by her

unwed mother: 'I went in (to the Foundling Hospital) Jewish, but I came out Catholic.' On the other hand, Protestant charities usually placed Catholic and Jewish children in Protestant homes.[5]

The many cases where a child's name or religion was changed caused further loss of identity. Not only was the child separated from his or her family, but having his or her grounding characteristics changed added to the loss of the child's sense of self.

Riding the Trains

The first group of 37 children train riders from New York City took a boat to the train station in Albany, New York, on September 28, 1854. Once in Albany, nine more children were added to the group. All 46 children boarded a train heading to Dowagiac, Michigan.

CAS agent E. P. Smith accompanied the orphans on this first train ride. In his journal, he wrote of the journey. He explained the cacophony of immigrant accents heard as the orphan group made its way through the station. There were Italian, Norwegian, German, and Irish voices. Initially, a train conductor told Smith he and the group of orphans would have their own train car, but that did not happen. Smith wrote about how the group ended up crammed onto the train:

> We are finally pushed into one [train car] already full—some [orphans] standing, a part sitting in laps, and some on the floor under benches—crowded to suffocation, in a freight-car without windows—rough benches for seats, and no back—no ventilation except through the sliding doors, where the little chaps are in constant danger of falling through.[6]

There were no lights on the trains at night because electric light had not been invented yet. No one was allowed to get off the train until it had reached the final destination in Michigan, so there was a bathroom rigged inside for the ride. The children shared their crammed car with numerous other passengers. Smith stated he would not write about the worst acts he

Railroad Lingo

Special terminology was used to refer to the small towns along the railroad tracks: whistle-stops, tank towns, and roundhouses. Whistle-stops were the places where the train stopped just long enough to blow the whistle. A tank town had either a pond or water tower where the steam-powered trains could fill up their tanks. And a roundhouse was a turntable that the steam engine could be loaded onto and then spun around to face the opposite direction. After using the roundhouse, a train that had been going east could turn around and head west.

witnessed of other people on the train, not the worst of which were swearing and drinking whiskey. One passenger even had a fire going in a corner of the train car, which added smoky, thick air to the already challenging situation. The uncomfortable ride lasted approximately four days.

THE SELECTION PROCESS

When the train arrived at the final destination, Dowagiac, the children put on their new outfits from their suitcases. News of their arrival had already spread. Advertisements had been placed in local papers.

For the selection to begin, the children were herded to a central stage in the town and told to step up onto a crate for inspection. When farmers inspected an orphan boy, they often checked to see if the boy's muscles were adequate for doing demanding farmwork. The farmers wanted strong and healthy children who could work and would not be a burden.

After that first train stop, there were nine children who had not been chosen. So, the rest of the children got back on the train and went farther down the line to other towns to keep searching for homes. After a while, two boys were left, then none. This became the standard practice for the orphan trains, which spread the children out to small towns mostly along the train route. In some cases, farmers heard about the children and drove in from a distance to see about adoption.

Screening Applicants

Of that first orphan train's placements, applicants for children were not well screened. All that was required to adopt a child was a letter of recommendation from the local clergy or justice of the peace.

For later train placements, a committee of local leaders was organized to screen and recommend applicants who wanted children. The committee was made up of doctors, lawyers, clergymen, business owners, and others who were respected members of the town. This way, when the orphan train arrived, there

The Placing-Out Selection Process

Orphan train rider Hazelle Latimer was sent west at age 11. As an old woman, Latimer looked back on the selection process: "That was an ordeal that no child should go through. They pulled us and pushed us and shoved us. . . . This old man came up and his mouth was all stained brown and I thought, well, he'd been eating chocolate candy or something. Then he said, 'Open your mouth.' I looked at him and he— 'I want to see about your teeth.' I opened my mouth and he stuck his finger in my mouth and just—and rubbed over my teeth. And his old dirty hands just—I wanted to bite, but I didn't."[7]

were people waiting and ready to choose a child. However, the CAS was not involved in the screening of applicants. Also, the children did not have a say in whom they would be living with. So, children sometimes went to homes that were not a good fit for them. These early placements were an experiment in re-homing children. The experiment had positives and negatives.

Brace worried that poor children
would grow up to become beggars and thieves.

Many orphans were placed with farm families.

EARLY SUCCESSES
AND FAILURES

The orphan train program was not without risks. CAS agents took the children from the city, placed them in farm homes out of state, and then left. Some agents lived in rural areas in the Midwest, but most went back to New York. The

CAS's goal was to check on children several times during the first year after placement to see how they were doing with their new families, but this usually did not happen. Instead, an agent might check on a placed child once during the first year or the child or foster parent might write a letter to the CAS communicating how the placement was working out.

In 1871, the CAS's assistant secretary was J. Macy. He wrote approximately 8,000 letters to follow up on placements each year. But he heard back from only a fraction of the families, approximately 2,000. Often, children could not write to the CAS because they did not know how to write. They may also have had trouble writing letters without their adoptive parents seeing the contents.

As a result of these obstacles, the placement failure rate and news of problematic placements was not easily or accurately reported. Additionally, the CAS wanted to present a positive picture of their programs to raise money to keep them going. So, the actual success rate of the orphan train placements is unknown. But the CAS was glad to receive letters about positive placements. One former orphan wrote:

*I have a good mother and father. . . . I am learning a lot.
. . . When I came [to Iowa] I did not know how to take the
halter off the pony and did not know how to harness or hitch
up a horse. I do now.*[1]

POOR PLACEMENTS

Unfortunately, not all children were happy with their placements. Some farmers treated the children as laborers and worked them long hours and did not feed them much. Though the CAS advertised that adopted children could be used as extra farmhands, this was not what Brace had envisioned for the children. Brace had hoped the children would become part of loving families

A Placing-Out Agent

In 1900, the CAS hired Reverend Herman Devillo Clarke as a full-time placing agent. Every year, he traveled thousands of miles to do follow-up visits on children. Clarke was born in New York, but he moved several times to where he was most needed. Sometimes, a placement would not work out and he would have to retrieve the child. If he did not have another suitable option for the child, he would take the child home with him. This was a frequent occurrence. Clarke wrote about one such occasion with a girl ill with TB. She told Clarke, "'Oh, Mr. Clarke, I don't want to be toted about any more.' [Clarke] replied, 'My dear girl, you shall not be any more. You are to have the very best home and stay always.' [Clarke] was speaking of heaven."[2] The girl died within a week.

Clarke and his wife had three children of their own. Clarke died in 1928, one year before the official end to the orphan train movement. He was 78 years old.

while they were learning a trade and life skills. That way, the children could become productive members of society instead of turning to lives of crime and poverty.

Some children were abused in their new homes. Orphan train rider George Spence was one of these children. His story made the local newspaper in Beloit, Wisconsin. Spence rode the train when he was just three years old and arrived in Milwaukee, Wisconsin. John Pacala, a farm laborer, stole Spence out of the train car when it arrived. Pacala beat the boy for ten years. Some of the abuses young Spence suffered were later explained by the superintendent of the Humane Society, Mr. Clayton:

> Mr. Clayton said young Spence had been made to work hard by Pacala, who had frequently lifted him in the air by his ears and held him there for several minutes, and had beaten him with whips and with a sawed off ball club, the top of which was filled with lead. He said the boy's body was a mass of bruises and cuts. [3]

Spence was appearing in juvenile court on an unrelated charge of theft, when the judge for the case saw the boy's injuries: "Judge Neelen noticed his red and swollen ears and his apparent hesitancy in

Young boys ready for their journey west stand in front of the CAS central office in New York City

talking as he looked at his guardian."[4] After the judge asked Spence about his injuries, the boy testified about the abuse. Spence was taken from Pacala and sent to a detention home to live. Had the boy not been in court because of his stealing, the physical abuse might never have been discovered. Rural farms of the time could be quite remote and isolated. Because of this, it is impossible to report how often such abuses occurred. Children did not always put up with such abuse. Sometimes, teenagers ran away from abusive situations.

Conversely, the public often feared having children from the city moved to their small towns. Many saw the orphan trains as bringing crime from the city to the country, and the country people often did not trust the relocated children.

DISCRIMINATION IN PLACEMENTS

There is some dispute about whether there was discrimination among the placements. Although some scholars claim the orphan trains were devoid of discrimination of any kind, others record that the white Protestant boys were clearly favored in the CAS placement programs.

Some of this discrimination could have been the result of families wanting children who shared their religious and ethnic background. Immigrants, such as Irish and Jewish children, with cultural

Immigrant children were often seen as less desirable than children who were born in the United Sates.

upbringings and customs different from those looking to adopt, were often ignored. And because boys were thought to be better laborers on farms, girls were often passed up by potential adopters. There were also complaints from Catholic and Jewish groups that the CAS was placing children of those religions with Protestant families for conversion purposes. Race discrimination was also an issue. The CAS was started before the American Civil War (1861–1865), when slavery was still legal, so African-American children were even less likely to be placed or helped by the CAS.

More Options for Orphans

To combat discrimination, other organizations similar to the CAS were started, such as the Colored Orphan Asylum, opened in 1836, and the Hebrew Orphan Asylum, which opened in 1860. In later years, the CAS did place more African-American children. This increase in placements and the financial support the organization received were

Songs and Storytelling

At the time of the orphan train movement, traditions and legends were passed down to other generations through songs and storytelling. The poor and orphans were often reflected in those songs. One folk song, "The Orphan Girl," was shared with the Missouri Folklore Society by C. H. Williams from Bollinger County. It went, "Twas cold and dark and the snow fell fast, But the rich man shut his door, And his proud lips curled as he rudely said, No home, no bread for the poor."[5]

indications that public support for helping these minority classes was growing.

In its beginning years, the CAS did not include African-American orphans on the orphan trains.

New York City police often brought abandoned babies to the CAS.

BABY TRAINS BEGIN

he CAS had a good program in place for finding homes for orphaned children, but the organization had another problem to tackle. There were many babies and toddlers who were orphaned as well. This was a challenge for the CAS.

Because younger children and babies could not help much on a farm, the CAS could not attract midwestern farm families as easily as they had for older children.

Unwanted Babies

The biggest problem, however, for unwanted babies was not whether they would be adopted. It was infanticide. Infanticide is murdering of an infant or very young child. Historically, this has been a problem faced by many societies. During the orphan train movement, infanticide occurred mainly because of economic problems—the family could not afford another mouth to feed, so the child was killed. There is no way of knowing how common or rare infanticide was because babies that were disposed of were not always found.

Another way unwanted babies were handled was by vendue, an

Preferred Children

Mr. Swayne, one of the placing agents for the CAS, summed up traits prospective parents some-times requested: "The predominating preference is for children with blue eyes and blonde curly hair. The only request ever made for one with red hair that I know of was from a farmer in Indiana. He and his wife had red hair, and they had three red-headed little girls. They wanted a red-headed boy."[1]

auction. People would bid for a baby, and the lowest bidder would get the child. The bid represented how little the bidder thought he or she could spend on food and clothing for the child for one year.

Other unwanted babies were simply abandoned. Those babies were called foundlings. The term comes literally from abandoned babies being found. When families were poor and could not care for all of their children, they sometimes would leave babies in a basket on someone's doorstep. Receptacles were even set up as places where people could leave a baby and know that it would be taken in by a church or other such charitable organization. The babies were also found discarded in garbage dumps. Sometimes, a parent would attach a note to a baby's clothing explaining the circumstances or begging that a good home be found for the child.

Asylum at Last

On October 11, 1869, Sister Mary Irene Fitzgibbon and the Sisters of Charity of Saint Vincent de Paul started the New York Foundling Asylum in a brownstone on East Twelfth Street in New York City. This asylum was set up to take in babies who had been abandoned because of the

American Civil War. The war created more orphans and abandoned children when the mothers could no longer care for them. The name of the organization was later changed to the New York Foundling Hospital. It helped fill an important gap in the orphan train movement by caring and finding homes for babies and toddlers. By January 1870, within a few months of opening, the hospital had taken in 123 babies.

The hospital moved twice before ending up on East Sixty-Eighth Street. In 1871, the organization raised money for a second building and received $100,000 from the city and from public donations. The hospital raised $71,500 for the

The Civil War

The Civil War created more orphans that would need placement because their parents died or were left homeless after war ravaged the country. During the Civil War, more than 620,000 soldiers died out of the 3 million who fought. Of those who died, many were parents who left behind children.

The war was fought between the North and the South, the division between the northern and southern areas of the United States. Each side was fighting for the rights of their own states and how those rights compared to the union of states as a whole. General Robert E. Lee led the soldiers fighting for the South, while Ulysses S. Grant led those fighting for the North. The North's win made Grant popular with many Americans. He later ran for president of the United States, was elected, and served two terms. Abolishing slavery was one part of the Civil War and was an important step in working toward humane treatment of workers. This spilled over to how orphans were treated.

cause. The new hospital included several buildings and took up an entire city block. The organization hired wet nurses to breast-feed the babies, a physician helped care for the children, and the sisters ran the hospital. The hospital was well regarded because it had a low mortality rate. This was because new arrivals were quarantined to make sure diseases would not spread among the babies. Sister Teresa Vincent took over as director of the Foundling Hospital when Sister Mary Irene died in 1896. Sister Teresa became mother superior of the hospital and instrumental in its operation.

A DIFFERENT PLACEMENT PROCESS

Initially, the hospital planned to take in and care for the babies. The Foundling Hospital also made efforts to keep families together. The hospital changed its initial policy of having abandoned babies placed in

Note Left by a Mother

A mother attached a note dated July 1870 to her baby before abandoning him at the hospital. It read: "To the Sisters of the House, Necessity compels me to part with my darling boy. I leave him, hoping and trusting that you will take good care of him. . . . God only knows the bitter anguish of my heart in parting with the little dear; still if it costs me my life I am obliged to give him up."[2]

cribs outside the hospital to having the cribs inside the hospital. They hoped this would encourage the mothers to come in and perhaps agree to continue nursing the child while the child stayed in the hospital. The sisters also hoped the mother would be able to take the child back at a later time, when she had gotten back on her feet financially.

Later, the number of babies grew so high that the hospital decided to follow the CAS's model of using trains to send the children to new homes. The main difference between the Foundling Hospital's trains and the CAS's orphan trains was that prospective parents requested babies from the hospital beforehand, so the babies were sent out on the trains for a specific family. With the CAS, children were sent out on trains and then viewed for prospective adoption without knowing whether they would be adopted or by whom. Another

Mortality Rates

Mortality, or death, rates among infants in the nineteenth century were high, as much as 30 percent. These deaths were mostly due to intestinal problems. The Foundling Hospital, under the direction of Sister Mary Irene, had great success in improving mortality rates because it used wet nurses. This allowed the children to be breast-fed, providing them with better nutrients. The Foundling Hospital's mortality rates were relatively low at 19 percent because of the nursing system. Other foundling hospitals had death rates as high as 76 percent during this same time period.

difference between the Foundling Hospital and the CAS was that the hospital tried to place babies with Catholic families, whereas the CAS left the choice of religion up to the adoptive parents.

People could apply to the Foundling Hospital for specifics such as hair and eye color and indicate if they wanted a boy or a girl. Then, a number was assigned to the adoptive parents, the number was stitched into the infant's clothing, and the child was sent on the train to the new parents. The parents would meet the train at the station and have their adoption number in hand like a receipt. Then, an agent would verify that the adoption number matched the number stitched into the clothing. The new parents would sign the appropriate paperwork, and the child would be theirs.

The First Baby Trains

In 1873, 20 years after the first orphan trains went west, the first baby train was sent to Maryland. This contrasted the way modern adoptions work in that the prospective parents were not interviewed and no home visits were done prior to adoption. A lot of the social work at the time was done on faith and goodwill.

As the movement went on, the baby trains carried even more children than the initial orphan trains. One newspaper article in 1910 noted,

> A whole carload of babies not one of whom was over three years old, passed through Chicago today on a 2,500 mile trip. . . . They were billed to Houston and San Antonio, Texas, where each will be adopted by a southern family.[3]

While the average orphan train carried 30 children, the baby trains usually moved more babies. Baby trains took infants west and south, whereas orphan trains took children mostly to western farms. Many baby trains placed children in Louisiana. One of the largest recorded moves of orphans was in 1909 when 300 children were taken to Loreauville, Louisiana.

With large numbers of babies needing homes, inventions such as the telephone would make

"Train Brings 18 Babies to Nebraska"

An article titled "Train Brings 18 Babies to Nebraska" ran in Omaha's *World-Herald* newspaper on December 15, 1921. It announced the arrival of a baby train: "The population of Nebraska was increased yesterday by eighteen souls when the modern stork, train No. 13 of the Rock Island, pulled into the Union Station with thirty-five of the most wonderful babies imaginable. These tots, ranging in age from twelve months to 5 years, former wards of the New York Foundling Hospital and now daughters and sons of Nebraska, Missouri and Kansas folks, presented a picture of happiness and good nature away out of proportion to the tedious ride almost across the continent. Eighteen of these children will be adopted into Nebraska homes."[4]

communications easier for the agents who wanted to schedule adoptions or to follow up on placed-out babies. By 1910, more than 27,000 children had been taken in by the Foundling Hospital.

An illustration in a newspaper depicting the New York Infant Asylum,
an organization much like the Foundling Hospital

Orphan train riders with two of the CAS's placing-out agents

THE MOVEMENT
CHANGES COURSE

After working with the CAS for 19 years, Brace wrote a book about the CAS's progress. In the introduction of *The Dangerous Classes of New York*, written on June 1, 1872, he concluded,

The cheapest and most efficacious way of dealing with the "Dangerous Classes" of large cities, is not to punish them, but to prevent their growth; to so throw the influence of education and discipline and religion about the abandoned and destitute youth. . . . To so change their material circumstances, and draw them under the influence of the moral and fortunate classes.[1]

PROGRAMS DEVELOPED FOR THE POOR

Brace realized that though the orphan trains were successful in many respects, moving children out of the city was not solving the problems of crime and poverty when immigrants kept flooding into the city. The ongoing immigration to New York ensured that joblessness and poverty would continue to fuel crime and the other issues he had been trying to remedy. Therefore, ongoing programs were needed to battle these issues. Brace believed educating people and reducing illiteracy would keep poverty and crime from increasing. Through the CAS, he achieved much in the way of accomplishing this goal.

In addition to lodging houses for orphans, the CAS began other programs in New York. The organization created a shelter for mothers and their children, nursery schools, playgrounds, and many other clubs designed to help the poor. Additionally, the CAS ran programs to keep people healthy by providing them with dental and medical care.

Seaside Retreat

Sea air was believed to be one of the best cures for the sick at the time. In the late 1800s, the CAS opened and operated vacation homes at the water's edge. The CAS had several vacation homes like this, including homes for sick mothers and children, disabled children, and poor children. These vacationers usually stayed at the houses from one to three weeks. The CAS hoped that seaside vacations would lift their spirits and improve their health.

Reading Rooms

The CAS also set up free reading rooms to give people another place to spend their time outside of the crowded tenements. One problem with the tenements was that they had grog houses in the buildings. This was like having a bar at home, which added to the alcoholism and poverty problems as people spent much of their earnings in the grog houses.

Brace wanted the impoverished people to have a place to go that did not serve alcohol, so the reading rooms sold only coffee. Initially, when the reading rooms were opened, people did come to them. But the numbers eventually fell off.

The CAS hoped to help people who lived in crowded tenements.

People preferred to read and spend their leisure time at home no matter how crowded or poor the circumstances.

New Leadership

In 1890, Brace died from kidney failure due to Bright's disease. At that time, Brace's two sons took on leadership roles in the organization. Charles Jr. took his father's place as secretary and Robert became the new director of emigration. Under this new leadership, the mission of the CAS changed from saving children to saving families. Along with this, the CAS stated its new central goal: "No child should be taken from its natural parents until everything possible has been done to build the home into a proper place for the child."[2] As a memorial to its founder and secretary, the CAS bought property outside of the city and named it the Brace Farm School.

BRACE FARM SCHOOL

Through the years, the CAS noticed that some placements failed because the children did not fit in to farm life and working on a farm. To prevent this problem, the CAS started the Brace Farm School in 1894 just outside New York City in Valhalla, New York. At the Brace Farm School, children were trained for two to three months in farmwork then sent on an orphan train for placement. This increased their success rate dramatically because the children went to the farms with appropriate skills and expectations.

Theodore Roosevelt

WHITE HOUSE CHILD WELFARE CONFERENCES

In 1909, the White House held its first
Conference on the Care of Dependent Children
to address issues for children and youth. President

Theodore Roosevelt, along with 200 other conference attendees, proposed nine plans for children. The plans included foster care, foster home inspections, education, and medical programs for foster children. The message from this conference was that children should be moved away from institutionalization and kept with their families. If a child could not be kept with his or her family, then he or she should be placed in nearby foster care. The 1909 conference also set a trend for sharing information between agencies to help one another.

The Great Depression

As the orphan train movement was near its end, the country fell into the Great Depression, on October 29, 1929, when the stock market crashed. This date would be forever known as Black Tuesday. Everyone wanted to sell their stocks, but they could not find buyers. People were going bankrupt from the losses. They tried to get their money out of the banks, where some had left it for safekeeping, but even the banks were going broke because they had invested much of the money they were holding into the stock market as well.

The Depression lasted until the early 1940s. Millions of Americans could not find work. With the prosperous years of the Industrial Revolution over, people no longer felt they could take in another mouth to feed. They simply could not afford to assume responsibility for orphans.

The railroad cars became a place people jumped onto to get free rides to other towns as they went in search of work. People of all ages, including entire families, rode the trains illegally for this purpose. The economy did not turn around until the United States entered World War II (1941–1945) following Japan's attack on Pearl Harbor, Hawaii, on December 7, 1941.

In 1919, the White House Conference on Standards of Child Welfare was held. President Woodrow Wilson and attendees worked in committees to wrestle with several issues: child labor, children with special needs, and medical options for mothers and children. Also in 1919, the Conference on the Care of Dependent Children was held. At this conference, a new bureau to help address these issues was formed—the Bureau for Exchange of Information Among Child-Helping Agencies.

In 1921, this bureau became the Children's Welfare League of America. Conferences were held every ten years to discuss topics related to children's welfare. As a result of these ongoing conferences, the government passed laws and worked to improve conditions and standards for children and families over the years.

CHANGING LABOR FORCE AND ECONOMY

Several events led to the end of the orphan train movement. On October 29, 1929, the stock market crashed and marked the beginning of the Great Depression.

Penicillin Discovered

In 1928, a Scottish scientist named Alexander Fleming discovered penicillin. This strong antibiotic could treat many of the illnesses that plagued society during the orphan train era. The discovery saved many lives, which thereby reduced the amount of parents dying and leaving children orphaned.

The state of the US economy made it hard to find families willing to take in a child, which would be another mouth to feed. Many states also passed laws forbidding interstate placement of children. This was the greatest factor in the end of the movement. Michigan passed the first such law in 1887. Later, the state added to the regulation by passing a law to charge a bond for any child brought into Michigan by the CAS. Other states followed suit.

These laws were passed because children were taking jobs from adults who needed the work. Additionally, many people still felt the train riders were undesirables. They believed the orphan trains relocated potential criminals to their states.

In addition to states passing laws preventing the placement of children across state lines, other legislation was passed to prevent child labor. Demand for labor in the West also declined. With the laws becoming stricter and demand for labor lessening, there were fewer places for the orphan trains to travel. One of the last recorded orphan trains was sent to Texas in 1929. The movement officially ended in 1930.

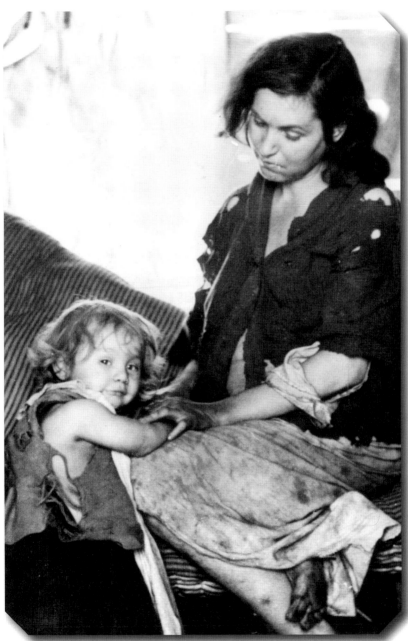

*The Great Depression made families less likely
to be able to adopt an orphaned child.*

Orphans attended a horse show in New York City in 1913.
The orphan trains gave many young people a chance at a different life.

Legacy of
the Train Riders

The Kansas History of Orphan Trains Web site reports that there are approximately 2 million living descendents from the orphan train riders. This number is staggering considering the challenges of mortality these orphans would have faced staying in New York, either living on the streets or in disease- and poverty-stricken slums. The orphan trains and emigration west gave these children a chance at a different future.

In 2010, one source estimated that only 100 orphan train riders were still alive. Even the youngest of the remaining orphan train riders would be in their early eighties.

Success Stories

Perhaps the most famous orphan train riders are Andrew Burke and John Brady. As adults, both men were elected governors: Burke of North Dakota and Brady of Alaska. Burke was four when he was orphaned and taken in by the CAS. After his placing-out to an Indiana farmer, Burke became a drummer boy in the Civil War. As governor of North Dakota, he discovered a glitch in the state's laws that did not allow North

America's Most Wanted Reunited Siblings

In 1989, the popular television program *America's Most Wanted* aired a special episode trying to reconnect a train rider with her parents. Sylvia Wemhoff had been relocated as a baby. Right after the show aired, the Orphan Train Heritage Society got many calls, but none were the reconnection Wemhoff had hoped for. The show was rebroadcast several months later. That time, Wemhoff's brother, Joseph, called in and the brother and sister were reunited after being apart for 70 years.

Dakotans to vote during presidential elections. Burke got a new law passed and the state's citizens helped vote Grover Cleveland into office in the next election.

Brady was a three-term governor of Alaska. He was adopted by a judge who described him as "the homeliest, toughest, most unpromising boy in the whole lot." The judge added, "I had a curious desire to see what could be made of such a specimen of humanity."[1]

A train rider who ended up in Missouri also became successful in government. Henry Lee Jost was initially fostered by a Nodaway County judge. Jost was a farmer's apprentice before becoming a hired hand when he was 15 years old. He used the money he earned from farming to put himself through law school, became a prosecuting attorney for Jackson County and then a two-term mayor of Kansas City. After that, he served in the US Congress.

Many other train riders also went on to lead happy lives. In addition to becoming governors, some went on to work in other professions and notable positions. According to the CAS's Web site, there was "one congressman, one sheriff, two district attorneys, three county commissioners as well as numerous bankers, lawyers, physicians, journalists, ministers, teachers and businessmen."[2]

ADOPTION AND FOSTER CARE TODAY

As a result of the orphan train movement, the CAS, and other children's programs, many laws have been passed protecting the rights of children and families. These laws affected not only the placement of children in foster and adoption situations but also areas such as public education, child labor, nutrition, health care, and vocational education.

Perhaps the legacy of the orphan train movement is its recognizing the importance of keeping families together, if possible, rather than pulling them apart. The decisions

A Leader in Preservation

In 1986, Mary Ellen Johnson of Springdale, Arkansas, was researching orphan trains for a local history project. She visited with a man who was a former orphan in his living room and listened to his story of living in a New York orphanage. The man said all he could see out of his narrow window at the orphanage was the Statue of Liberty. Johnson was so moved by his story she searched for any information on the orphan train riders and made that her life's work from that day forward.

That same year, Johnson founded the Orphan Train Heritage Society of America. The nationwide organization acts as a clearing-house for historical information about the train riders. The society has a museum in Concordia, Kansas, with a variety of artifacts. It is the only museum of its kind in the United States.

Children may now travel from one country to another to become part of a family.

made to move children out of bad situations and go forward with placements were always difficult. Modern adoption and foster care follow efforts to keep children with biological parents unless the environment will be harmful to the child. Those decisions are scrutinized much more carefully now and subject to judgment and investigation by government agencies. There is also a trend toward trying to keep siblings together. Some adoptive families adopt all siblings to keep the children together. In November 2010, a Minnesota couple announced plans to adopt nine boys from a family in the Philippines. The couple had already adopted two other children from the family and wanted to adopt the other siblings because they felt so strongly about keeping them together.

The Legacy Remains Alive

Though the orphan train movement ended in 1930, the legacy of the orphan trains is still felt today. For many, it is a subject of controversy. These brave children who set out on an adventure to the unknown to start new lives had sometimes chosen the trip willingly and other times not. The CAS and its placing-out program were criticized. There were good and bad consequences of this early relocation program. For some children, the trip west gave them a chance at healthy and safe lives. Others were placed in situations that were more harmful than their previous lives in the city.

Regardless of the mixed placements, what resulted was the largest emigration of children from the East to the West that the nation has ever seen. No one knows, of course, what fate these children would have met had they stayed in the city. But the legacy of the train riders remains alive in their 2 million descendants spread out across the United States and the laws and institutions now in place to help children and families in need.

Placing-Out in Britain

After World War II, Great Britain shipped approximately 150,000 orphans, between the ages of three and 14, abroad. Most of these children were sent to Canada and Australia. The event was seen as a shameful and embarrassing chapter in British history. Many of the children expressed anger and hurt at being sent to another country so far from their homeland.

A women holds her adopted child from Haiti on December 22, 2010.

TIMELINE

early 1850s

There are approximately 30,000 homeless children in New York City.

1853

Charles Loring Brace founds the Children's Aid Society (CAS).

1862

A lodging house for girls is opened.

1862

On July 1, 1862, President Abraham Lincoln signs the Pacific Rail Act. It approves government funding for the railroad expansion.

1869

On October 11, the Sisters of Charity of Saint Vincent de Paul start the New York Foundling Asylum in New York City.

1854

The first lodging house for newsboys opens in New York City.

1854

In September, the first orphan train travels from Albany, New York, to the Midwest. The first stop is Dowagiac, Michigan.

1858

A new lodging house with 250 beds is opened for boys.

1873

The first baby train goes to Maryland.

1873

According to one study, 40 percent of the 3,000 children placed by the CAS this year have one or both parents living.

1887

Michigan is the first state to pass a law that forbids interstate placement of children.

Timeline

1890	1894	1899
On August 11, Brace dies.	The CAS opens the Brace Farm School is Valhalla, New York.	On July 22, 1899, the newsboys of New York strike against the two publishing giants of the time: William Randolph Hearst and Joseph Pulitzer.

1919	1929	1930
The White House Conference on Standards of Child Welfare is held.	One of the last orphan trains travels to Sulphur Springs, Texas, on May 31.	The orphan train movement officially ends.

1909

President Theodore Roosevelt calls the first White House Conference on the Care of Dependent Children.

1909

In one of the largest recorded moves of orphans, 300 children are taken to Loreauville, Louisiana.

1910

The New York Foundling Hospital has taken in more than 27,000 children.

1986

Mary Ellen Johnson founds the Orphan Train Heritage Society of America.

2003

The Orphan Train Heritage Society of America begins building a museum in Concordia, Kansas, to help orphans research their origins.

2010

Approximately 100 orphan train riders are still living.

ESSENTIAL FACTS

DATE OF EVENT

1854 to 1930

PLACE OF EVENT

❖ The Children's Aid Society was founded in New York City.

❖ The first orphan train traveled to Dowagiac, Michigan.

❖ The orphan train movement placed orphans in 47 of the 48 US states. No orphans were placed in Arizona.

KEY PLAYERS

❖ Charles Loring Brace

❖ Sister Teresa Vincent

❖ Sister Mary Irene Fitzgibbon

❖ Mary Ellen Johnson

❖ orphans and children

❖ newsboys and bootblacks

HIGHLIGHTS OF EVENT

❖ The objective of the orphan trains was to get homeless children off the streets of New York City and place them in loving homes, primarily farms in the Midwest. Brace believed children were better off being taken in by families and working for the family rather than being raised in institutions such as the orphan asylums that were previously used to house these homeless children.

❖ The children who rode the orphan trains were orphaned because their parents had died in wars or because of disease, they came from impoverished families unable to support them, or they had parents who had other issues, such as alcoholism, which made them unable to care for their children.

❖ More than 250,000 children were relocated by the CAS. The exact number of orphans relocated is not known due to sealed or lost placement records.

❖ The orphan train movement lasted 76 years and was the largest emigration of children in the United States. This movement was also the beginning of formal foster care in the United States.

QUOTE

"When a child of the streets stands before you in rags, with a tear-stained face, you cannot easily forget him. And yet, you are perplexed what to do. The human soul is difficult to interfere with. You hesitate how far you should go."—*Charles Loring Brace*

GLOSSARY

adopt
> To take on parental responsibilities for a child.

agent
> An adult who traveled with children to find them new homes.

almshouse
> A place for needy people who cannot support themselves to live, also a poorhouse.

bootblack
> A boy who shines shoes to earn a living.

descendant
> A person with the same ancestry as those who were born before him or her.

divinity school
> A professional school for students studying religion.

emigrant
> Someone who moves from one place within a country to another place.

foster care
> To take in a child who needs to be cared for and become the guardian.

foundling
> A baby or toddler who is found after being abandoned or left by the parents.

immigrant
> Someone who moves from one country to another.

indentured servant
> One who is contracted to work for someone in return for room and board, until a certain age, usually 18.

lodging house
> A place where children could rent a room and get a meal.

newsboy
> A boy who worked to earn a living selling newspapers on street corners.

orphan
> A child without parents.

orphanage
> An institution to house large numbers of children.

placing-out
> A system to move children from the city to homes in the country.

prospective
> Possibility, as in a possibility to find a new home for a child in need.

prostitute
> One who sells one's body for sexual acts in exchange for money.

slum
> A run-down area of a city where poor people live.

tenement
> Crowded apartment housing in poverty-stricken areas.

vagrant
> One who wanders and does not have a home.

workhouse
> An institution where people who cannot afford rent can live and work to pay for a place to sleep.

ADDITIONAL RESOURCES

SELECTED BIBLIOGRAPHY

Brace, Charles Loring. *The Dangerous Classes of New York.* New York: Wynkoop & Hallenbeck, 1872. Print.

Brace, Charles Loring. *The Life of Charles Loring Brace, Chiefly Told in His Own Letters.* Ed. Emma Brace. New York: Scribner's Sons, 1894. Print.

O'Connor, Stephen. *Orphan Trains: The Story of Charles Loring Brace and the Children He Saved and Failed.* New York: Houghton Mifflin, 2001. Print.

FURTHER READINGS

Warren, Andrea. *We Rode the Orphan Trains.* New York: Houghton Mifflin Harcourt, 2004. Print.

Wendinger, Renèe. *Extra! Extra! The Orphan Trains and Newsboys of New York.* Sleepy Eye, MN: Legendary, 2009. Print.

Web Links

To learn more about the orphan trains, visit ABDO Publishing Company online at **www.abdopublishing.com**. Web sites about the orphan trains are featured on our Book Links page. These links are routinely monitored and updated to provide the most current information available.

Places to Visit

Louisiana Orphan Train Museum
233 South Academy, Opelousas, LA 70570
337-948-9922
http://laorphantrain.com
The museum has genealogical information about train riders and their descendants available for visitors, as well as artifacts from the era.

National Orphan Train Complex
300 Washington Street, Concordia, KS 66901
785-243-4471
http://www.orphantraindepot.com
The National Orphan Train Complex is dedicated to preserving the stories and artifacts from those who rode the orphan trains from 1854 to 1929. The museum is open to visitors year-round.

SOURCE NOTES

Chapter 1. Dire Conditions

1. *American Experience: The Orphan Trains*. Dir. Janet Graham, Edward Gray. 1995. Film. Transcript online. 31 Oct. 2010.

2. Ibid.

3. Ibid.

4. Ibid.

5. Stephen O'Connor. *Orphan Trains: The Story of Charles Loring Brace and the Children He Saved and Failed*. New York: Houghton Mifflin, 2001. Print. 107.

6. "Newspaper Accounts: Want Ads Placed in Kansas Newspapers." *Orphan Trains of Kansas*. 9 Dec. 1910. Web. 22 Nov. 2010.

7. *American Experience: The Orphan Trains*. Dir. Janet Graham, Edward Gray. 1995. Film. Transcript online. 31 Oct. 2010.

8. Ibid.

Chapter 2. Charles Loring Brace

1. Warren W. Wiersbe, comp. *Treasury of the World's Greatest Sermons*. Grand Rapids, MI: Kregal, 1993. Print. 97.

2. Stephen O'Connor. *Orphan Trains: The Story of Charles Loring Brace and the Children He Saved and Failed*. New York: Houghton Mifflin, 2001. Print. 32.

3. PBS. "About the Program." *American Experience: The Orphan Trains*. WGBH Educational Foundation, 2009. Web. 20 Nov. 2010.

4. Stephen O'Connor. *Orphan Trains: The Story of Charles Loring Brace and the Children He Saved and Failed*. New York: Houghton Mifflin, 2001. Print. 48.

5. Charles Loring Brace. *The Life of Charles Loring Brace, Chiefly Told in His Own Letters*. Ed. Emma Brace. New York: Scribner's Sons, 1894. Print. 154.

6. Stephen O'Connor. *Orphan Trains: The Story of Charles Loring Brace and the Children He Saved and Failed*. New York: Houghton Mifflin, 2001. Print. 45.

7. Ibid. 52.

8. Charles Loring Brace. *The Life of Charles Loring Brace, Chiefly Told in His Own Letters*. Ed. Emma Brace. New York: Scribner's Sons, 1894. Print. 82–83.

9. Charles Loring Brace. *Hungary in 1851, with an Experience of the Austrian Police.* New York: Scribner, 1852. Print. 348.

10. Charles Loring Brace. "Walks Among the New-York Poor: Rotten Row." *New York Times.* 19 Apr. 1853. Print. 2.

11. Charles Loring Brace. "Walks Among the New-York Poor." *New York Times.* The New York Times, 24 May 1854. Web. 28 Feb. 2011.

Chapter 3. Homeless Children

1. Diane Ravitch, ed. *The American Reader: Words That Moved a Nation.* New York: HarperCollins, 1990. Print. 302.

2. Children's Aid Society. "Our City Charities No. IV." *New York Times.* 7 Apr. 1860. Print. 1.

3. Stephen O'Connor. *Orphan Trains: The Story of Charles Loring Brace and the Children He Saved and Failed.* New York: Houghton Mifflin, 2001. Print. 47.

4. Charles Loring Brace. "Walks Among the New-York Poor." *New York Times.* The New York Times, 28 Sept. 1853. Web. 23 Feb. 2011.

5. "Juvenile Crime Reported: A Juvenile Stabbing Affray." *New York Times.* The New York Times, 26 May 1869. Web. 23 Feb. 2011.

Chapter 4. Newsboys and Lodging Houses

1. Stephen O'Connor. *Orphan Trains: The Story of Charles Loring Brace and the Children He Saved and Failed.* New York: Houghton Mifflin, 2001. Print. 89.

2. David Nasaw. *Children of the City.* Garden City, NY: Anchor/ Doubleday, 1985. Print. 167.

3. "A Returned Street Boy's Speech." *New York Times.* 16 Jan. 1875. Print. 8.

Chapter 5. The Solution: Orphan Trains

1. Charles Loring Brace. "Walks Among the New-York Poor." *New York Times.* The New York Times, 27 Jan. 1854. Web. 23 Feb. 2011.

2. Charles Loring Brace. "Walks Among the New-York Poor." *New York Times.* The New York Times, 19 Apr. 1853. Web. 23 Feb. 2011.

SOURCE NOTES CONTINUED

3. Charles Loring Brace. "Walks Among the New-York Poor." *New York Times*. The New York Times, 17 May 1859. Web. 23 Feb. 2011.

4. *American Experience: The Orphan Trains.* Dir. Janet Graham, Edward Gray. 1995. Film. Transcript online. 31 Oct. 2010.

5. Marilyn Irvin Holt. "Orphan Train Genealogy." *Ancestry Magazine*. Jan./Feb. 1995. Ancestry.com. Web. 10 Feb. 2011.

6. Charles Loring Brace. *The Dangerous Classes of New York & Twenty years work among them.* New York: Wynkoop & Hallenbeck, 1872. Print. 249.

7. *American Experience: The Orphan Trains.* Dir. Janet Graham, Edward Gray. 1995. Film. Transcript online. 31 Oct. 2010.

Chapter 6. Early Successes and Failures

1. Marilyn Holt. *The Orphan Trains: Placing Out in America.* Lincoln: U of Nebraska P, 1992. Print. 56.

2. Clark Kidder. *Orphan Trains & Their Precious Cargo: The Life's Work of Rev. H.D. Clarke.* Westminster, MD: Heritage, 2001. Print. 56.

3. "Taken Off Orphans' Train To Life Of Bitter Cruelty: George Spence, Beaten With Heavy Club, Sent to Detention Home." *Ancestry.com*. Beloit Daily News, 27 Nov. 1908. Web. 16 Nov. 2010.

4. Ibid.

5. Michael D. Patrick and Evelyn Goodrich Trickel. *Orphan Trains to Missouri.* Columbia: U of Missouri P, 1997. Print. 53.

Chapter 7. Baby Trains Begin

1. "Foundlings Find Homes." *New York Times*. 15 May 1901. Print. 2.

2. National Orphan Train Complex. "New York Foundling Hospital Letters." 22 Nov. 2010.

3. Marilyn Holt. *The Orphan Trains: Placing Out in America.* Lincoln: U of Nebraska P, 1992. Press. 113.

4. "Train Brings 18 Babies to Nebraska." *The World-Herald.* NEGenWeb, 15 Dec. 1921. Web. 22 Nov. 2010.

Chapter 8. The Movement Changes Course

1. Charles Loring Brace. *The Dangerous Classes of New York & Twenty Years Work Among Them.* New York: Wynkoop & Hallenbeck, 1872. i–ii.

2. Paul J. Ramsey. "Wrestling with Modernity: Philanthropy and the Children's Aid Society in Progressive-Era New York City." *New York History.* New York State Historical Association, 2007. Web. 21 Nov. 2010.

3. "Quotations from the speeches and other works of Theodore Roosevelt." *Theodore Roosevelt Association.* n.p., n.d. Web. 21 Nov. 2010.

Chapter 9. Legacy of the Train Riders

1. *American Experience: The Orphan Trains.* Dir. Janet Graham, Edward Gray. 1995. Film. Transcript online. 31 Oct. 2010.

2. "The Orphan Trains." *The Children's Aid Society.* The Children's Aid Society, n.d. Web. 21 Nov. 2010.

INDEX

ABOUT THE AUTHOR

Kristin F. Johnson teaches college writing and lives in Minnesota. Johnson has won several writing awards, including the Loose-Leaf Poetry Series Award, the Loft Literary Center's Shabo Award for Children's Picture Book Writers, and the Mystery Writers of America Helen McCloy Award.

PHOTO CREDITS

Kansas State Historical Society, cover, 3; Mary Evans Picture Library/Alamy, 11, 96 (left); National Orphan Train Complex, 6, 78; Hulton Archive/Getty Images, 15; Library of Congress, 16, 19, 28, 31, 36, 39, 77, 96 (right), 98 (top); Oscar Gustav Rejlander/Getty Images, 27; Archive Photos/Getty Images, 35; Lewis W. Hine/Getty Images, 41; Picture Collection, The New York Public Library, Astor, Lenox and Tilden Foundations, 45; Andreas Feininger/Time & Life Pictures/Getty Images, 46; J. Burke/Getty Images, 57; Wallace G. Levison/Time & Life Pictures/Getty Images, 58; Jacob A. Riis/Getty Images, 62, 98 (bottom); Lewis W. Hine/Museum of the City of New York/Getty Images, 64; George Eastman House/Getty Images, 67; The Art Archive/Alamy, 68, 97; Jacob A. Riis/Getty Images, 81; AP Images, 83, 99; MPI/Getty Images, 87; Bain News Service/Library of Congress, 88; Manu Fernandez/AP Images, 92; Jacques Brinon/AP Images, 95